Little Scientists, BIG Questions

What Does a Vet Do?

Written by Ruth Owen and Designed by Alix Wood

WINDMILL BOOKS

Published in 2025 by Windmill Books,
an Imprint of Rosen Publishing
2544 Clinton St.
Buffalo, NY 14224

Cataloging-in-Publication Data

Names: Owen, Ruth.
Title: What does a vet do? / Ruth Owen.
Description: Buffalo, New York : Windmill Books, 2025. | Series: Little scientists, big questions
Identifiers: ISBN 9781538395332 (pbk.) | ISBN 9781538395349 (library bound) | ISBN 9781538395356 (ebook)
Subjects: LCSH: Veterinarians--Juvenile literature. | Veterinary medicine--Juvenile literature. | Pets--Health--Juvenile literature.
Classification: LCC SF756.O94 2025 | DDC 636.089--dc23

Image Credits:
Alamy: 13T (Alexandru Tomatu), 13C (Alexandru Tomatu), 14 (Parker Photography), 19B (Image Broker), 21 (Australian Associated Press); IstockPhoto: 18 (Banks Photos), 20 (Urbancow); Ruby Tuesday Books: 2–3, 15T; Shutterstock: CoverT (Prostock-Studio), CoverB (maxbelchenko), 2–3 (Photojulia/Vasily Kovalev/frantic00/Anakumka/Eric Isselee), 4 (Magnifical Productions), 5 (Juice Flair), 6 (Pressmaster), 7 (Svett/Andrey Kuzmin/Svetlana Ray/Erik Lam), 8 (Pressmaster), 9 (SeventyFour/Tatiana Popova/maxbelchenko), 10 (decade3D), 11 (SciePro/decade3D/3D-Horse), 12 (Ermolaev Alexander), 13B (Erik Lam), 15B (cynoclub), 16 (Ngo Thye Aun), 17L (PeopleImages.com – Yuri A), 17R (olgaru79), 19T (Bruno Monico), 22 (Pixel-Shot/Todorean Gabriel), 23 (mariesacha/Eric Isselee).

Printed in the United States of America

CPSIA Compliance Information: Batch #CSWM25
For Further Information contact Rosen Publishing at 1-800-237-9932

Today, we are visiting the vet with our pets.

My owner thinks my tummy is getting bigger.

Vets are doctors who take care of animals.

They work in an animal hospital.

Vets are kind and caring and very good at **science**.

Come on, little scientists, let's answer that BIG question!

A vet asks the animal's owner lots of questions.

Is the animal eating?

Can the animal poop and pee?

Does the animal want to play?

Does the animal seem tired?

All scientists ask questions. Then they do investigations to answer their questions.

Let's Investigate!

A vet listens to an animal's heart and breathing with a stethoscope.

A healthy dog's heart should beat 80 to 120 times per minute.

A vet takes an animal's temperature with a thermometer.

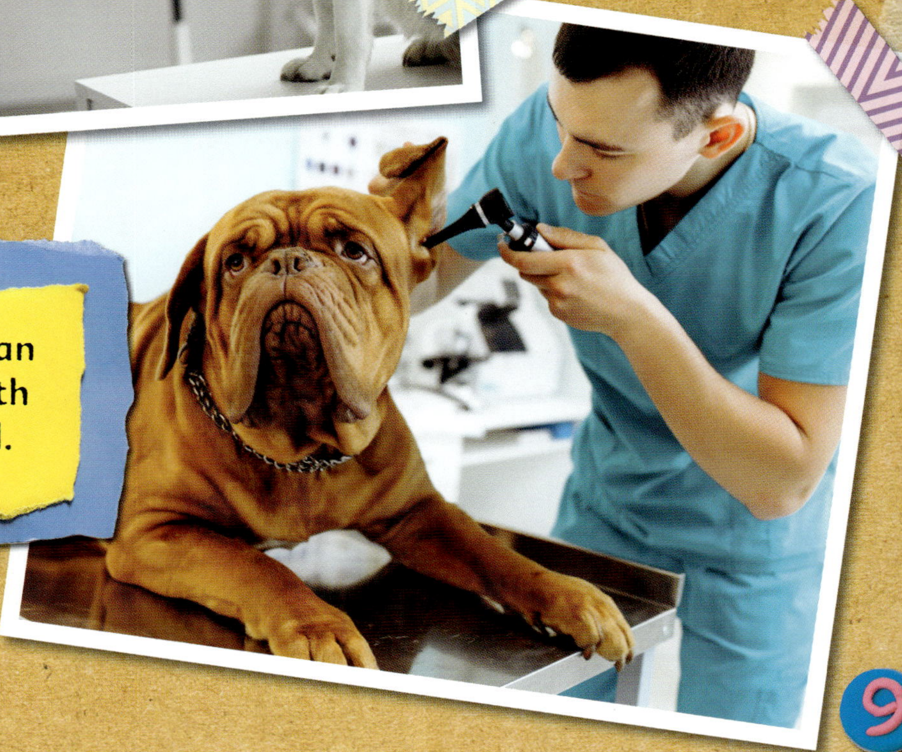

A vet looks into an animal's ears with an otoscope tool.

A vet must know all about anatomy.

An animal's anatomy is its bones, muscles, and other body parts.

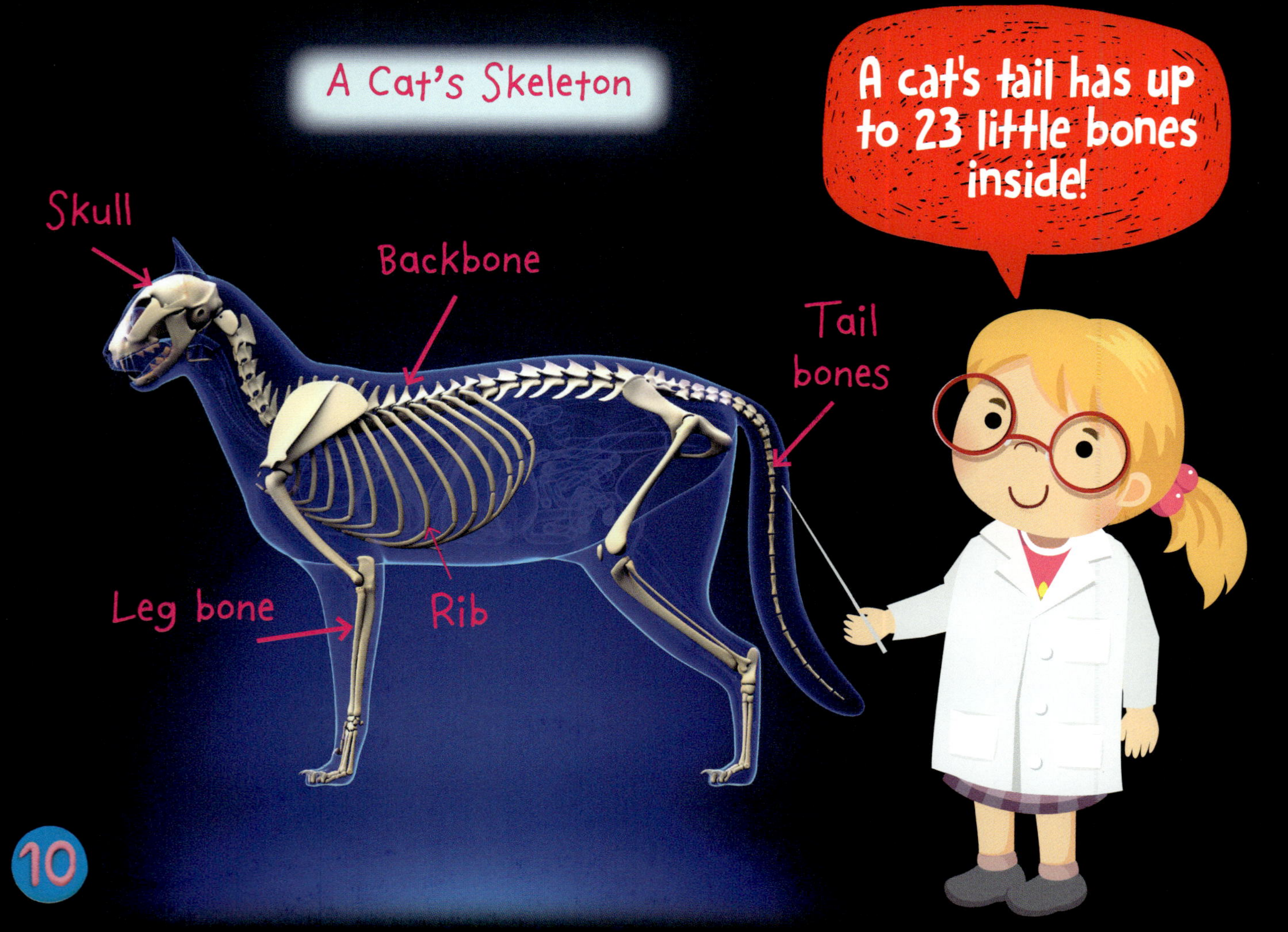

A vet must know the anatomy of lots of different animals.

Look at what's inside this horse!

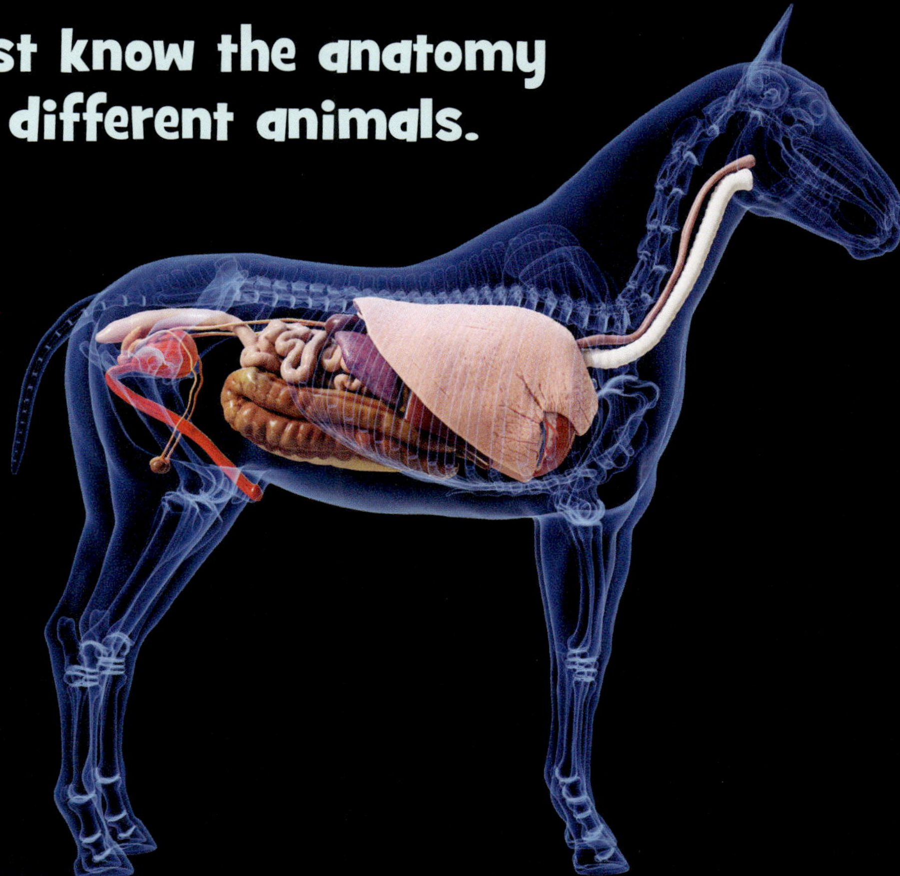

A dog's muscles

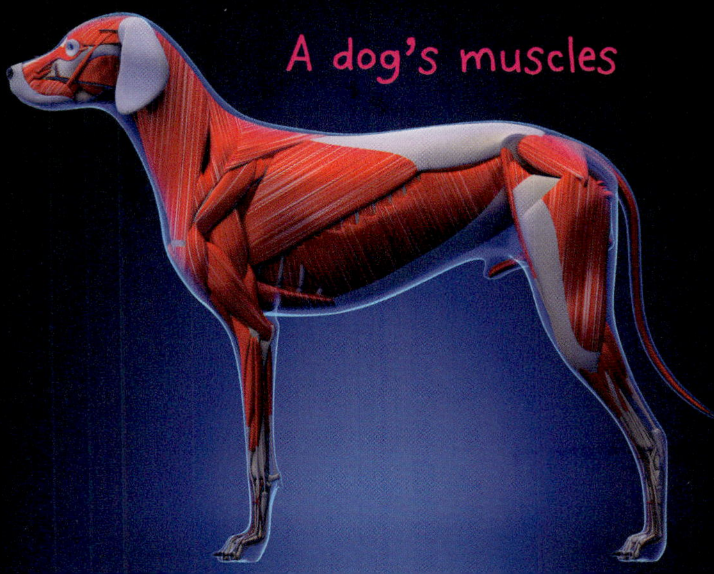

A tortoise's skeleton

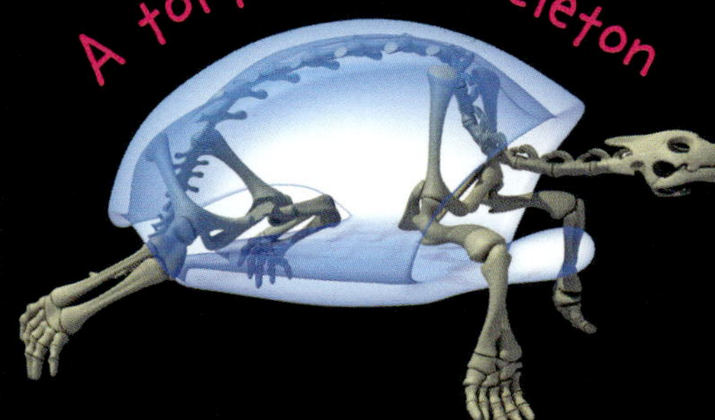

An X-ray machine is used to take a picture of what's inside an animal's body.

A vet gives the animal a special injection so it is sleepy and doesn't move.

A vet has important helpers called nurses or technicians.

The X-ray picture shows the dog has broken its leg.

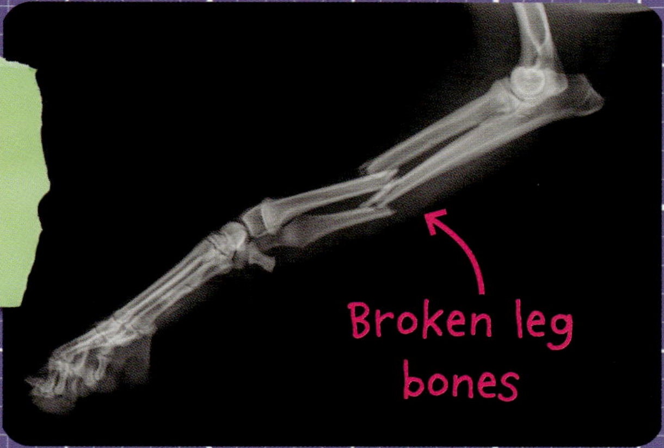

The vet uses screws and a special piece of metal to fix the broken bones.

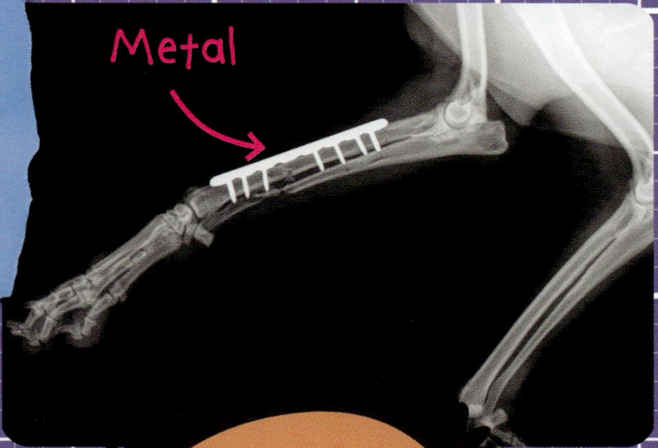

A vet also uses an ultrasound machine to see inside animals.

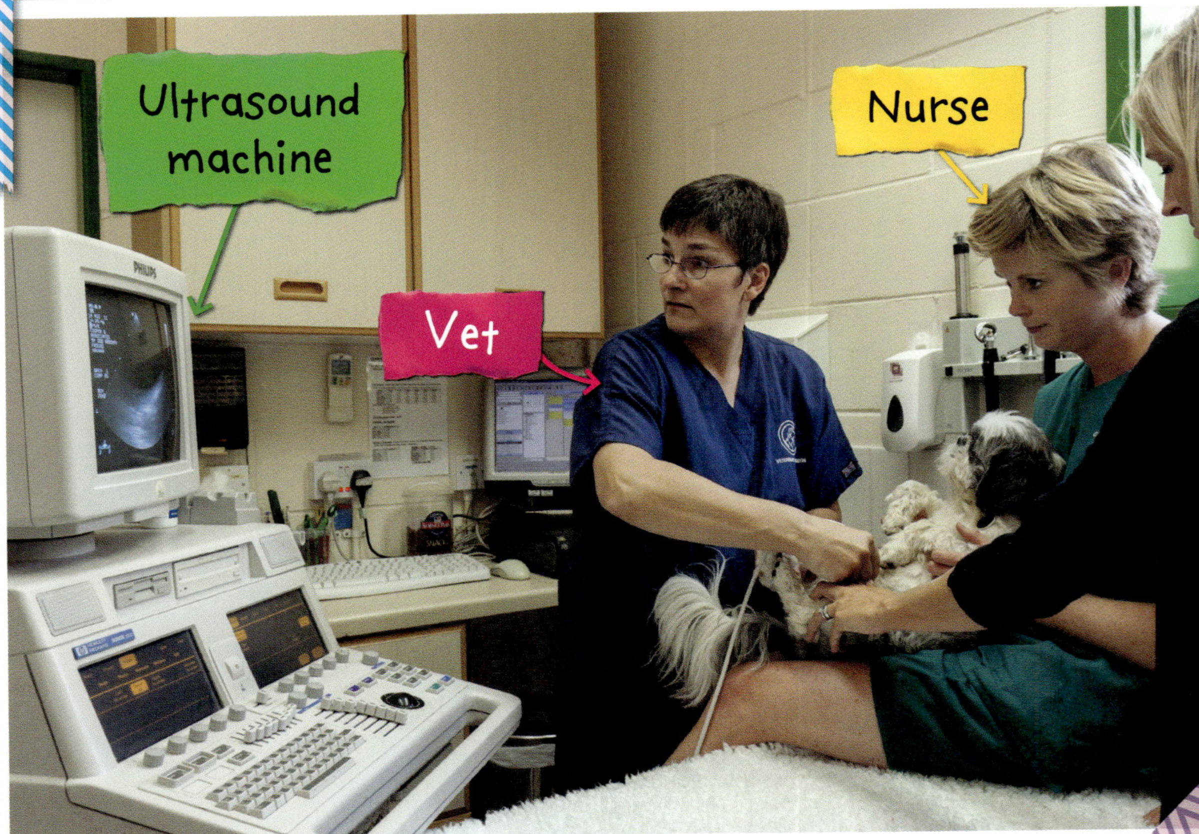

The vet puts a part called a probe on the dog's tummy.

There are 1, 2, 3, 4 puppies growing inside the dog.

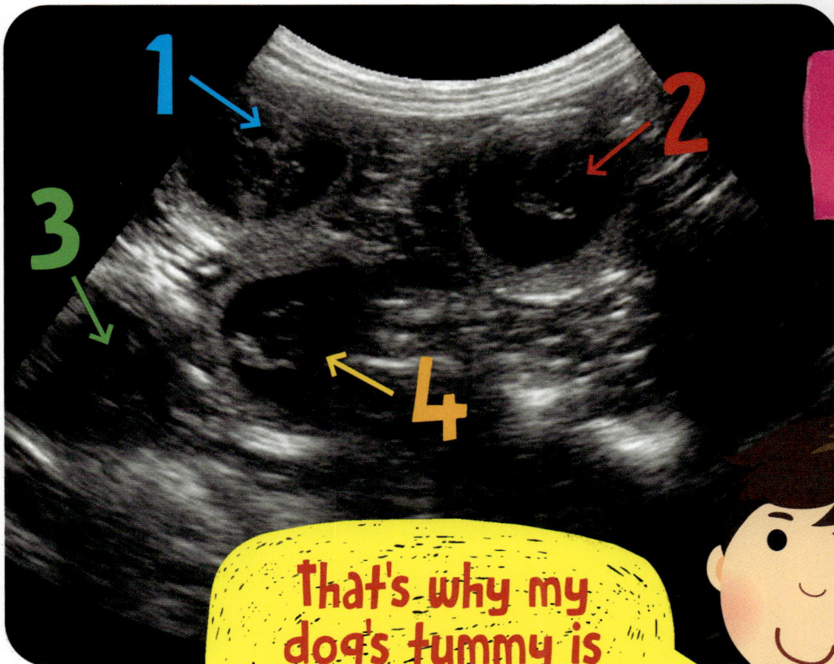

Ultrasound picture

Puppies

Sometimes poop can show a vet why an animal is sick!

This poor kitty is in the animal hospital.

A nurse collects some of the kitten's poop.

A technician looks at a tiny bit of poop under a microscope.

The kitten is sick because she has roundworms living in her stomach.

The vet will give the kitten medicine to kill the worms.

This cat is having an operation to remove a painful tooth.

The vet gave the cat an anesthetic to make her go to sleep. The drug also keeps her from feeling pain.

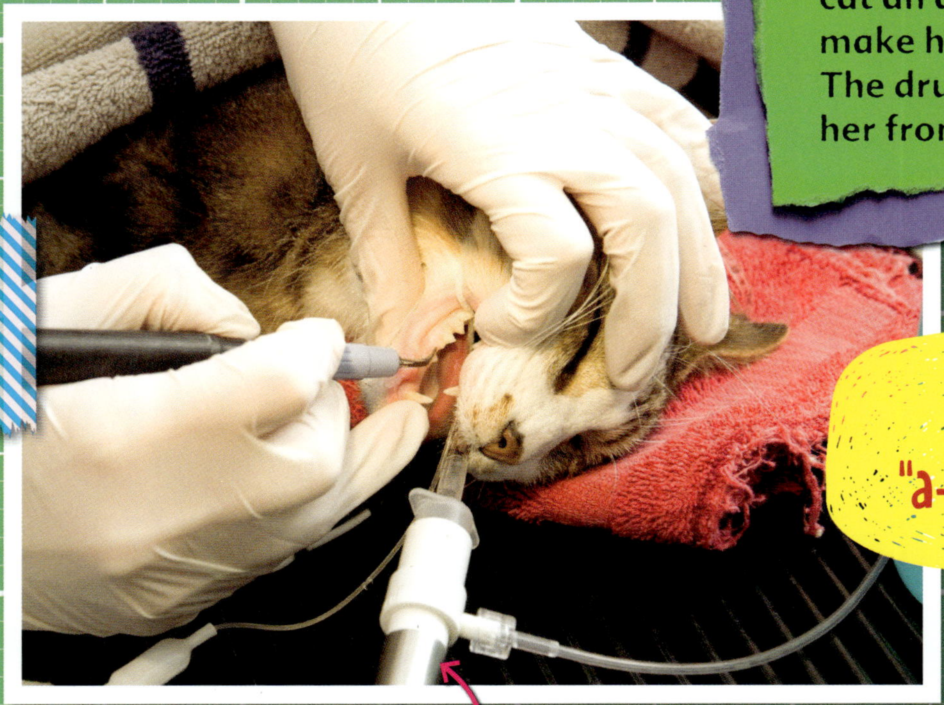

The cat breathes in anesthetic through this tube.

After an operation the animal is put in a hospital cage.

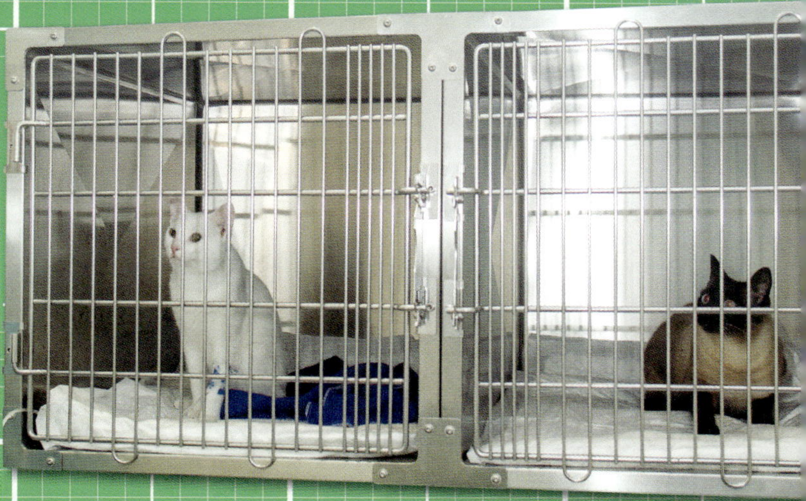

A nurse puts a warm blanket over the cat.

Sometimes vets use their science skills to help big animals on farms.

A vet is also an animal dentist.

Some vets take care of the animals in zoos.

A vet uses math to carefully measure how much medicine to put in an injection.

Vets help us take care of our pets.

The vet injects a microchip with a special number into this puppy.

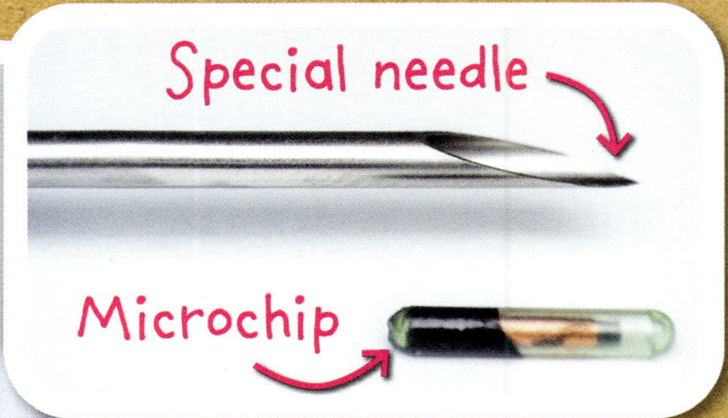

If the puppy gets lost and then found, a vet can read the number with a machine.

Vets and nurses clip animal toenails. Long toenails can hurt an animal's feet.

The vet gives the rabbit an injection called a vaccination. It will keep him from catching nasty rabbit diseases.

Let's say it!
"vak-suh-NAY-shun"

Now we know how vets use science.

Good work, little scientists!

My Science Words

anatomy
All the parts of a living thing. An animal's anatomy includes its bones, muscles, heart, and stomach.

investigation
A careful look at something to discover facts about it.

temperature
How hot or cold something is. An animal's temperature shows a vet if the animal is healthy or sick.

vaccination
A special medicine or injection that keeps an animal or person from getting a disease.

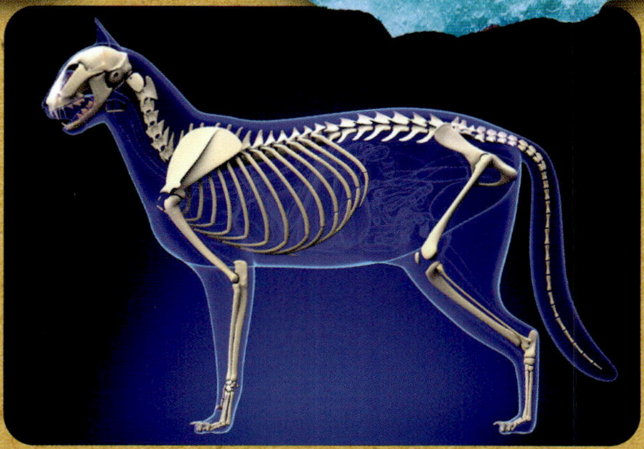